The Greatest Teacher of All!

"JESUS in 100 Ways" Series

Papa & Mama Goose

The Greatest Teacher of All!
"JESUS in 100 Ways" Series

Papa & Mama Goose

Copyright © 2020
Enchanted Rose Publishing
P.O. Box 991
Hempstead, TX 77445

Published by Enchanted Rose Publishing
Layout by Cynthia D. Johnson @
www.diverseskillscenter.com

Written by Papa & Mama Goose

Printed in the United States of America
ISBN-13: 978-1-947799-74-5

I can remember many teachers who have helped shape my life.

My mother was my first teacher. She taught me my first words and later how to take care of myself.

Mom taught me how to love and do good to others.

Dad taught me lessons like how to fix things that are broken around the house.

He taught me to be strong and take responsibility for my actions.

My siblings are my teachers as well. They teach me by the good example they try to set.

Sometimes they make wrong choices, but I forgive them and give them another chance to be my example.

My Bible School teachers are some of my favorites because they teach me about GOD.

Our Bible School teachers want us to grow in our Love and knowledge of JESUS.

When I read my Bible, I learned that I am reading the mind of GOD.

JESUS is my Greatest Teacher of All!

JESUS gave a powerful sermon on the mount.

The message must have sent a shockwave through the listeners.

They had never heard things like being merciful, peace makers, and hungering and thirsting after righteousness (Matthew 5:1-48).

JESUS taught people to Love GOD and their brothers. He also taught people to forgive others because GOD forgives us.

JESUS taught us to master our flesh and live by the SPIRIT of God.

I have decided to follow JESUS...The Greatest Teacher of All.

Scripture References

Matthew 7:24-27; Luke 5:46-49; 1 Corinthians 3:10-11; Ephesians 2:19-22

The Greatest Teacher of All!

"JESUS in 100 Ways" Series

Written by Papa & Mama Goose

Copyright 2020

by

Mama Goose Books

Hempstead, Texas

Papa & Mama Goose Media

Through the power of their faith and instructions from GOD's HOLY SPIRIT, these humble servants of CHRIST take us back to our beginning...The Bible. Although Papa and Mama Goose have written a plethora of books, none can hold a candle to how the WORD of GOD has guided their lives. Realizing that life on Earth is temporal, Papa and Mama Goose wanted to write Books about the Bible that would provide a Biblical Foundation for young children. The goal of the books is to teach youngsters to know and fall deeply in Love with GOD.

It was during their years in college that Papa and Mama Goose found CHRIST. They were taught the Gospel and baptized into the Prairie View CHURCH of CHRIST at Prairie View A & M University in Prairie View, Texas. Papa and Mama Goose enjoy sharing the same spiritual birthday. Currently, the dynamic duo are faithful members of the Fifth Ward CHURCH of CHRIST in Houston, Texas.

Follow Me On...

 Facebook

www.facebook.com/gomamagoose

 Twitter

@GoMamaGoose

 Instagram

MamaGoose Paris

gomamagoose@gmail.com

www.ingramcontent.com/pod-product-compliance
Lightning Source LLC
Chambersburg PA
CBHW041241040426
42445CB00004B/108